CAREER
&
EMPLOYABILITY

A Practical Guide to Building a Successful Future at Work

Jason Soh

Published by Scola Books
An imprint of Sunway University Sdn Bhd

No. 5, Jalan Universiti
Bandar Sunway
47500 Selangor Darul Ehsan
Malaysia

press.sunway.edu.my

ISBN 978-967-5492-68-6

Perpustakaan Negara Malaysia   Cataloguing-in-Publication Data

Soh, Jason
CAREER & EMPLOYABILITY : A Practical Guide to Building a Successful Future at Work / Jason Soh.
ISBN 978-967-5492-68-6
1. Career development.
2. Personnel management.
3. Applications for positions.
I. Title.
650.14

Edited by Hani Hazman
Designed and typeset by Rachel Goh
Printed by Vinlin Press Sdn Bhd, Malaysia

All information in this publication is correct at the time of printing and may be subject to changes.

Cover image: Master1305/Shutterstock.com
Image used under licence from Shutterstock.com

CONTENTS

FOREWORD

After graduating, many young people look forward to starting on the careers of their choice and being successful at their chosen vocation. To achieve success, one must of course be willing to work hard, maintain focus, and continually increase their knowledge and skill set.

As with all aspects of life, one must first set their priorities before starting anything. Here I am reminded of a quote by Stephen Covey, author of *The Seven Habits of Highly Effective People*, who said, "The key is not to prioritise what's on your schedule, but to schedule your priorities".

In this regard, I trust our young graduates will find this book most handy as it aims to provide them with valuable knowledge and understanding to prepare them for their careers. In the current ever-changing world, preparation is key to achieving success. I am sure students will gain valuable insights from the author, Jason Soh, who has had many years of experience teaching Career and Enterprise subjects, as well as Accounting and Finance. A dedicated lecturer who aims to create positive impacts in his students' lives, his book should undoubtedly provide added insights for those just venturing out into the working world.

This practical guide is easy to understand and a must-read for all students.

Professor Elizabeth Lee
Chief Executive Officer
Sunway Education Group

Personal and Social Competencies

1

Competencies and Skills

1. The terms "competencies" and "skills" are often used interchangeably as both refer to abilities you acquire from experience or training.

2. However, the two concepts are markedly different:

   - **Competencies**
     These are intangible yet observable qualities or traits that help you succeed in your job. A competency can be made up of various abilities, experiences and knowledge.

   - **Skills**
     These are specific abilities you learn to do a job well. These can range in complexity from welding to performing surgery. Employers can determine whether your training and experience prepare you for a specific job based on your skills.

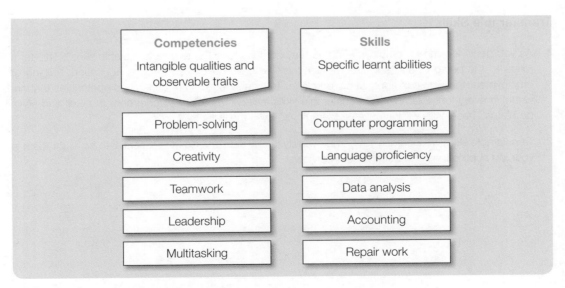

Competencies	Skills
Intangible qualities and observable traits	Specific learnt abilities
Problem-solving	Computer programming
Creativity	Language proficiency
Teamwork	Data analysis
Leadership	Accounting
Multitasking	Repair work

Figure 1.1   Competencies versus skills

Personal and Social Competencies

1. Your traits, behaviours and attributes can influence your employability as they allow you to work well with others.

2. To map your future pathway and develop into an enterprising and dependable person, you need to recognise your **personal and social competencies** that can be applied to future work environments. Your values and beliefs will strongly influence these competencies.

    - **Personal competencies**
      These reflect your inner self, personality and values. Personal competencies are demonstrated through tasks or activities that you are naturally good at and enjoy doing. This natural ability or interest to do something is called aptitude. With training, aptitude can be shaped into valuable work skills.

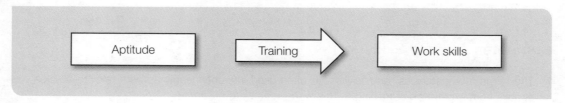

Figure 1.2   Companies often use aptitude tests to determine employability and training needs

    - **Social competencies**
      These reflect your abilities to deal with people and social situations. Social competencies are slightly different from personal competencies, which focus on the self rather than others. Your personality, experience and involvement in social events will help develop your social competencies, which are vital for networking. Understanding cultural differences is also essential when interacting with people of diverse backgrounds.

Transferable Skills

1. As you begin looking for employment, you may come across the term "transferable skills". This term refers to the personal and social competencies you have developed through education, training or employment that you can apply at a workplace. Transferable skills are general competencies that are useful in every job. Examples of transferable skills include the ability to communicate well and solve problems. These skills will increase your employability in the industry.

2. Transferable skills will increase your employability in any industry. So, it is essential to highlight them in your job applications and during your interviews!

Exercise 1.1 Competencies Coding

1. Look through the list of competencies and examples in the table below. You may already possess some of the competencies listed.

2. Develop a key for the different categories of competencies. For example, you could use four different colours or symbols to represent different categories:

   Red: Very good
   Blue: Can do
   Green: Would like to develop
   Grey: Does not apply to me

3. Now, code the list of competencies in the last column of the table according to your key.

4. You might like to do further research and add competencies that are not in the table.

Competency	Example	Colour
Working with a team	Working with others on a group project; helping a new student settle into your class	
Working with numbers	Saving pocket money or wages; balancing a bank account	
Being creative	Writing stories; designing using computer graphics; painting; drawing	
Staying fit	Practising and playing sports	
Communicating with others	Listening and talking to friends and teachers respectfully; conveying messages to others clearly	
Developing technological skills	Operating a smart device; using a computer	
Planning and organising	Arranging a team for a local competition	
Information gathering and researching	Finding information for a school assignment	
Problem-solving	Solving puzzles; overcoming issues with a schoolmate	
Designing new things	Creating handicrafts; designing clothes	
Assembling or repairing things	Repairing tyre punctures; assembling a small machine	
Learning new skills	Picking up new dance steps; learning how to play football	
Managing	Managing time, money, or people	
Following instructions	Following a recipe to prepare a meal	
Showing initiative	Getting on with things without having to be told	

Reflection 1.1 Competencies Checklist

Use this sheet to keep an up-to-date list of your competencies.

1. Look at the competencies you have already worked through in the previous table.

2. Now, complete this checklist by writing down all the things you are very good at.

My personal competency	How I learnt and currently apply this competency	A job that requires this competency

My social competency	How I learnt and currently apply this competency	A job that requires this competency

2 Professional Competencies

Learning Objective

Identify professional competencies and understand their link to career development

Professional Competencies

1. Professional competencies refer to the skills, knowledge, and traits valued by professional bodies and organisations related to your future career. All occupations require you to develop these competencies and apply them to the job.

2. However, some jobs require you to be more developed in certain **employability skills** and **industry-specific competencies** than others.

   - **Employability skills**
     These are the core traits and transferable skills valuable in nearly every job. You develop employability skills through education, training and work experience. Even while interacting with others through your hobbies and extracurricular activities, you develop and enhance many of the skills employers look for when deciding who they want to work with.

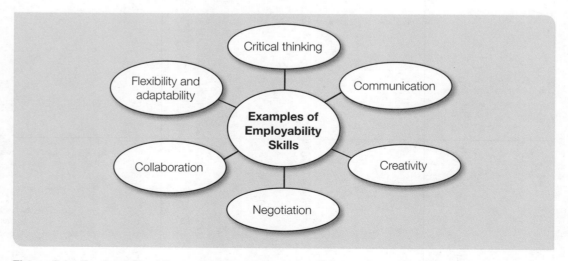

Figure 2.1 Employability skills are generic skills (not job-specific) that are needed in most work roles

- **Industry-specific competencies**
  These are developed by industry training boards and form the basis of competency-based training, such as the Vocational Education and Training and Technical and Further Education courses. You will need to show competence in tasks related to your specific industry or profession (such as accounting or computing).

Job Analysis

1. Job analysis is a systematic and detailed examination of jobs. It involves information gathering about a job through direct observation, questionnaires and interviews with current jobholders.

2. Companies perform job analysis from time to time to identify the duties and responsibilities that a job entails and the attributes, skills, and qualifications required.

3. The immediate outcomes of this analysis are **job descriptions** and **job specifications**, which help managers and human resource professionals recruit the best people, evaluate employee performance, and develop effective training programmes.

   - **Job descriptions**
     A job description shows an overview of the job's essential functions. It usually lists the job title, job position, location, duties to perform, reporting line and work environment. The general work skills and competencies (such as teamwork, problem-solving and communication) required may be set out in the job description.

   - **Job specifications**
     Job specifications detail the educational qualifications, work experience, training, specific work skills and personal characteristics needed to perform a particular job. Job specifications will also include the industry-specific competencies required.

Table 2.1   Job analysis is a complete and careful study of the knowledge, skills and experience needed to carry out a job effectively

Job Analysis	
Job Description	Job Specifications
1. Title, position, location	1. Education, work experience
2. Duties, reporting line	2. Training, skills
3. Work environment	3. Personal characteristics
4. General competencies	4. Industry-specific competencies

Exercise 2.1 Occupational Tasks

1. Choose an occupation you are interested in.

2. List 5–10 tasks that you would be required to perform as someone engaged in this occupation.

3. List down the employability skills and industry-specific competencies necessary for those tasks.

Occupation that I am interested in: (e.g. Graphic Designer)
_____

Tasks required to perform	Employability skills and industry-specific competencies
(e.g. Design)	(e.g. Creativity)

Tasks required to perform	Employability skills and industry-specific competencies

Exercise 2.2 Occupational Research

1. Research the occupation you are interested in.

2. Analyse its job description and job specifications.

3. What other additional information would you require as the job applicant?

Occupation that I am interested in: _____

Job description	Job specifications

Other additional information I need

3 Career Choice

The Holland Code Career Test

1. You can determine a potential career pathway that matches your personality type using a career pathway identification test. There are many types of tests available today, one of them being the Holland Code Career Test.

2. The Holland Code Career Test is a guide to gain insights into industries that suit your interest areas. It will help you narrow down an enormous list of careers to ones that match your personality.

3. The test is centred around **six career interest areas**—Realistic (R), Investigative (I), Artistic (A), Social (S), Enterprising (E), and Conventional (C). The test is also commonly known as the RIASEC Career Test.

Table 3.1 The Holland Code Career Test's six career interest areas and the corresponding career examples

RIASEC	Career field examples
Realistic (Doers)	Construction, outdoors
Investigative (Thinkers)	Science, engineering, academia
Artistic (Creators)	Creative arts, media, design
Social (Helpers)	Social and community services
Enterprising (Persuaders)	Business, sales, public service
Conventional (Organisers)	Accounting, finance

Source: Adapted from Holland (1985) and Truity (n.d.)

The Six Interest Areas

1. Each of the six career interest areas describes a cluster of related work tasks and activities.

2. People drawn to each of these interest areas tend to have specific characteristics, preferences, and personality traits in common.

Table 3.2   The six career interest areas of Holland's RIASEC profiling tool

Interest area	Description
Realistic	• Someone who likes working with their hands and bodies, working with plants and animals, and working outdoors • Involves the use of tools, machines or physical skills
Investigative	• Someone who likes working with ideas and concepts, and enjoy science, technology and academia • Involves theory, research and intellectual inquiry
Artistic	• Someone who likes working in unstructured environments and producing something unique • Involves art, design, language and self-expression
Social	• Someone who likes working in cooperative environments to improve the lives of others • Involves assisting, teaching, coaching and serving other people
Enterprising	• Someone who likes working in positions of power to make decisions and carry out projects • Involves leading, motivating and influencing others
Conventional	• Someone who likes working in structured environments to complete tasks with precision and accuracy • Involves managing data, information and processes

Source: Adapted from Holland (1985) and Truity (n.d.)

Personality or Career Tests

1. Personality or career tests evaluate your strengths, weaknesses, interests and skills. You can use them to help you explore career options and choose a career path compatible with your interests, skills and values.

2. Be mindful of the following when taking personality or career tests:
   - There are no right or wrong test results
   - Results from such tests are not 100% accurate. Be open to other possibilities.
   - Be honest in answering test questions to ensure your results are credible
   - Some tests or surveys are more reliable than others. Do check out which fits you best.
   - Results from such tests are just suggestions; they should not dictate what you are meant to do or be!

Exercise 3.1 The Holland Code Career Test

1. Complete the two surveys at the following links:
   - https://openpsychometrics.org/tests/RIASEC
   - https://www.truity.com/test/holland-code-career-test

2. Save your results from both surveys.

Group Activity

1. Discuss your survey results with your group. You can summarise the results of your group in the table shown on the following page.

2. How do you think your personality type and skills could help you work with others in a group? Create a mind map or table to show ways you could work in a group.

Name	Results	Characteristics

Name	Results	Characteristics

4 Self-Management Strategies

Learning Objective

Develop self-management strategies to enhance personal change and growth, including:

- Self-reflection
- Interaction with others through teamwork and networking
- Setting of SMART (specific, measurable, achievable, realistic, time-based) goals

Self-Management

1. Self-management is the ability to take responsibility for your behaviour and well-being so that you can make good decisions, set practical goals and achieve them independently. You can pursue a range of self-management strategies to achieve positive personal and career growth.

2. Some of the self-management strategies include the following:
   - **Self-reflection**
     Take time to think about and assess your thoughts, feelings, decisions and behaviours.
   - **Interaction with others through teamwork and networking**
     Develop self-management skills to let you communicate and interact efficiently with co-workers, supervisors or customers.
   - **Setting of SMART goals**
     Define an objective you want to achieve and devise an action plan to help guide and motivate you towards the goal.

Self-Reflection

1. Self-management involves controlling your actions as well as reactions. This can be improved through reflection.

> **NOTE**
>
> You have been doing a lot of self-reflection throughout this course! Can you identify how you have been flexing this muscle?

2. Some of the self-reflection strategies include the following:
   - Seek advice and feedback from others, including supervisors
   - Respond to constructive criticism
   - Evaluate your thoughts and actions and strengths and weaknesses
   - Modify behaviour to improve outcomes

Interaction With Others Through Teamwork and Networking

1. Interaction with others will enhance your personal and professional growth, which can help you improve your career prospects. This can be done via teamwork and networking.

2. Some of the strategies to improve your interaction with others include:
   - Recognising and improving your personal competencies
   - Developing your social competencies through team-building activities
   - Building a professional network
   - Having a career mentor
   - Working in team-based environments to cultivate collegiality

Setting of SMART Goals

1. To establish and achieve a successful career pathway, you should set goals to help guide your decision-making.

2. Effective planning and goal setting can be done using the SMART model. By setting goals that are **Specific**, **Measurable**, **Achievable**, **Realistic**, and **Timely**, you are more likely to stay focused, motivated, and on track.

Make your goals SMART	
Specific	**What is my goal?** • Identify a clear and concise goal • The goal should focus on the what, the how, and the who, if relevant
Measurable	**How will I measure whether I have achieved this?** • The measure could be a simple yes/no or pass/fail grading • Achievement could also be measured using qualitative or quantitative key performance indicators
Achievable	**What makes me think I can do this?** **What else do I need to do to achieve this?** • Goals should be set based on your skills and abilities • As personal and professional growth usually goes through a step-by-step progression, smaller and more specific goals should be identified
Realistic	**Is this the right goal for my career pathway development?** **How will I know?** • Goals must reflect your willingness and ability to achieve them • This depends heavily on your motivation and attitude
Timely	**What deadlines will I set and what review timeframes will I use to measure achievement?** • Deadlines help create focus and discipline • Timeframes could be reviewed and modified when necessary

Source: Adapted from Corporate Finance Institute (n.d.)

Figure 4.1   Setting SMART career goals

Exercise 4.1 SMART Goals

Complete your career SMART goals in the table below.

Specific	(e.g. I want to be a Professional Copy Editor in the next 10 years in the editorial sector of a renowned book publishing company.)
Measurable	(e.g. I will obtain a degree in English and Media and Communication studies and gain work experience as an Editorial Assistant, Junior Copy Editor and Proofreader.)

Achievable	(e.g. I am creative and detail-oriented, both character traits needed in the publishing industry. I also have a deep passion for books, which will be an advantage in my career.)
Realistic	(e.g. I am proficient in English and have consistently scored high marks in my English tests. I am also curious about knowledge and facts, a trait that can be useful when performing fact checks during editing.)
Timely	(e.g. I will obtain a degree in four years and have approximately six years of work experience as an Editorial Assistant, Junior Copy Editor and Proofreader.)

5 Strategies for Career Development

Self-Concept

1. Your self-concept (image) reflects your opinion of yourself as a person and how you think others perceive you. Learning about yourself will give you confidence and prevent you from making poor choices and unrealistic plans.

2. The better your understanding of yourself, the better your strategies will be, and vice versa. A good understanding of yourself would help you write a solid personal profile statement in your CV or résumé.

Personal Profile

1. A personal profile is a small paragraph at the top of your CV. It is a statement that describes you, your personal characteristics, skills, strengths, achievements and career goals.

2. It is helpful to match the job search with your personal profile and preferences. This helps ensure that the career choices suit your personality, interests and skills.

3. Your personal profile should include your work and life preferences, as well as your **T.A.C.K.S.**

I am a seasoned educator with many years of experience teaching students in international pre-university programmes. I possess strong interpersonal and organisational skills and demonstrate high professionalism and integrity in dealing with students and parents. I am also an expert in the subject matter that I teach and have received numerous accolades for my excellence in teaching.

Figure 5.1 A sample personal profile statement

Know Your T.A.C.K.S.

1. Your personal profile is the first thing potential employers or recruiters will read in your CV. So, it is essential to create a concise and robust introduction to your qualifications, skills and experience.

2. Your personal profile should include the following T.A.C.K.S.:

   - **Talents**
     Abilities you were born with (e.g. musical ability).

   - **Attributes**
     Qualities or features (e.g. helpful, courageous).

   - **Capabilities**
     Innate traits you bring to a task or situation (e.g. marketing, technological know-how).

   - **Knowledge**
     The understanding of concepts (e.g. science, law).

   - **Skills**
     Proficiencies developed through training or hands-on experience (e.g. communication, leadership, problem-solving).

Lifelong Learning

1. Lifelong learning refers to the different types of study and training on personal development, often self-initiated, that you might undertake throughout your life.

2. Advances in technology continually alter the structure of the industry and the economy, and both redundancies and skills shortages can occur. As a future employee, you will need to keep yourself up-to-date with ongoing professional development and training.

3. Lifelong learning encourages personal development and enhances your competitiveness and employability.

4. Some strategies to enhance your career development through lifelong learning include:

   - Completing work placements or doing volunteer and community work

   - Undertaking vocational training

   - Upskilling for professional development to facilitate career growth

Exercise 5.1 Me, Myself and I

1. What do you think your good points are?

2. What do those around you say your good points are?

3. List the answers to these questions in the table below. Then, compare what you think are your good qualities with what others think they are.

My good points	What do people around me say?

Exercise 5.2 T.A.C.K.S.

List your talents, attributes, capabilities, knowledge and skills in the table below.

Talents	
Attributes	
Capabilities	
Knowledge	
Skills	

6 Job Opportunities

Job Seeking

1. Job seeking requires a systematic and enterprising approach, often combining different methods to achieve desirable results. Contrary to the popular belief that the doors to job opportunities tend to open by chance, job seeking actually requires strategic planning.

2. Some job-seeking methods are more effective than others, depending on the type of work and the stage of your career. Nevertheless, it may also depend on your personality traits and, as some would say, chance.

Job Opportunities

1. Successfully finding a job starts with knowing where and how to look for one.

2. Sources of job opportunities include the following:

   - **Newspapers**

     This is the most traditional recruitment source. Employment vacancies are advertised in the classified section of newspapers. The classified section allows you to browse a variety of job advertisements easily and make quick comparisons.

Although newspaper advertising for vacancies, especially entry-level vacancies, is declining, many local opportunities are still advertised in regional and local newspapers. Examples of mainstream Malaysian newspapers with classified advertisements include *The Star* and *New Straits Times*.

- **Websites**

  Online employment websites are becoming the dominant method for attracting applicants. In Australia, the leading portals for sourcing employment include Seek (www.seek.com.au), All Jobs Australia (www.alljobs.com.au) and Careerone (www.careerone.com.au). In Malaysia, the mainstream job search portal is JobStreet (www.jobstreet.com.my).

  These sites offer the benefit of lodging résumés, finding job matches and receiving message alerts.

- **Professional associations**

  Employment agencies operate to source potential applicants and employees for organisations. They handle some or all of the recruitment processes for employers.

  In Australia, Australian Apprenticeship Centres and Group Training Organisations provide job opportunities through apprenticeships, while others like Youth Connections (www.youthconnections.com.au) focus on students at risk of not finishing school. In Malaysia, Recruiters Association Malaysia (www.recruitermalaysia.org.my) is a social medium for recruitment professionals that aims to reduce unemployment in the country.

- **Social and professional networks**

  Networking involves using your contacts, friends and relatives to help you find employment. Experts say networking is the most effective job-seeking method, as many positions are filled via recommendations.

  There are some potential advantages to networking:

  - You may acquaint yourself with established professionals in the industry
  - You may know about available job opportunities before they are publicly advertised
  - You may gain access to hidden job opportunities
  - You may be able to obtain direct contact information for the job

  Some strategies to build your networks include:

  - Identifying a **career mentor** or people you feel comfortable reaching out to for advice.
  - Establishing and expanding your professional social contacts through **e-networking**.

Career Mentor

1. A career mentor could be someone with relevant industry experience, a community leader or a counsellor who shares their knowledge and expertise to help you make informed career choices.

2. Career mentors could provide advice, tips, contacts, feedback, references and other support to assist you in job seeking.

E-Networking

1. E-networking is a way to connect with other professionals through social media platforms and e-networking sites such as LinkedIn. On an e-networking site, you can create a public profile and interact with other people in your industry and other related fields. Such sites allow you to connect with organisations, industries, and people who suit your career pathway.

2. Sometimes, employers or employees share job opportunities through online networks. However, e-networking sites are more suited for professional networking rather than for seeking entry-level jobs.

3. Some of the guidelines in using social media as part of your e-networking strategy include:

   - **Creating and managing a suitable professional digital profile**
     Consider your content carefully, as there may be consequences to what you post.

   - **Staying safe online**
     Ensure you protect yourself, your family, finances and devices from fraud or abuse.

   - **Communicating professionally**
     Be respectful of your audience and ensure you provide accurate information.

   - **Managing your privacy settings**
     Make choices about what gets shared and with whom it is shared.

Exercise 6.1 Job Opportunities

Identify job opportunities in the industry that you are interested in using four different sources.

Job title	Sources

Job title	Sources

Exercise 6.2 Career Mentor

Identify a suitable career mentor whom you could approach to help with job seeking. You can use the following prompts to help your answer:

- Who is the career mentor?
- Why can they be a suitable career mentor?
- How can they be a suitable career mentor?

_____

_____

_____

_____

_____

_____

_____

_____

_____

_____

_____

_____

_____

_____

_____

Exercise 6.3 E-Networking

Create a formal networking account on LinkedIn (www.linkedin.com) and share your link below.

URL: _____

7 Cold Canvassing

Learning Objectives

1. Recognise methods of finding job opportunities, including cold canvassing
2. Understand cold canvassing tips to improve your job-seeking chances

Cold Canvassing

1. Cold canvassing, or cold calling, is a method of job hunting where you take the initiative to approach potential employers by visiting or calling them directly. This is a method of putting yourself out there in an active manner, instead of just waiting for a door of opportunity to open.

2. Cold canvassing can be done through these methods:

   - **Face-to-face canvassing**
     Using the direct face-to-face approach to meet a potential employer.

   - **Letter canvassing**
     Mailing a canvassing letter to a potential employer.

   - **Phone canvassing**
     Calling a potential employer.

   - **Email canvassing**
     Sending an email to a potential employer.

   - **Social media canvassing**
     Using social media and electronic messaging to connect with a potential employer.

Tips to Perform Cold Canvassing

1. Cold canvassing prospective employers to ask for a job can be pretty effective. A cold call or visit in person at the right time may help you find job openings before they are advertised.

2. Effective cold calling requires the ability to politely and quickly get to the point.

3. The following are some pointers, advantages and disadvantages of cold canvassing methods:

- **Face-to-face canvassing**

Pointers:	Advantages:
• Canvass your network for potential opportunities • Start with a local organisation • Have a basic understanding of what the organisation does before approaching • Dress to match the expectations of the organisation	• If you make a good impression, you will be listened to because you demonstrate initiative and proactivity • You will get a quick response and resolution
	Disadvantage: • The process can be scary and intimidating (but very few people will chastise you for your efforts)

- **Letter canvassing**

Pointers:	Advantages:
• Tailor the letter specifically to the organisation • Find out the name of the person you are canvassing for the job position • Produce formal business letters following all the standard rules for formatting and style • Add your phone number and email address as part of your contact details on a single-page document	• You will show professionalism • You will be able to explain your skills and experience
	Disadvantages: • This method is less common nowadays, and letters rarely get read • If your letter is poorly written or too generic, the recruiter may not even bother reading it

- **Phone canvassing**

Pointers:	Advantages:
• Get contact details or a referral from someone in your career network • Call to learn about the organisation's application process or find out who you should contact • Enquire about work placement opportunities • Develop a script to help you in phone conversations	• You will have the opportunity to demonstrate your communication skills • You will improve your chances of getting the job if you talk to the right person
	Disadvantages: • You may not get through to the person you intend to talk to • Time is of the essence, and you are likely to be rejected upfront if the listener feels it is a waste of their time

- **Email canvassing**

Pointers:	Advantages:
- Prepare a formal, concise and straight-to-the-point email - Tailor the email to the organisation and address the appropriate contact person - Have a relevant title (header) to the email, which will not get rejected as spam - Send a follow-up email after a face-to-face or phone canvassing	- You can reach many potential employers - You can attach relevant documents to support your canvassing, such as your CV
	Disadvantages:
	- Your email may be treated as spam - Job-seeking emails can be perceived as a nuisance

- **Social media canvassing**

Pointers:	Advantages:
- Ensure your online profile is professional - Do not disclose too much personal information - Follow companies you are interested in and make insightful comments on their pages to show your interest and expertise - Put up posts asking about the job application process - Use private messages to communicate, rather than having a public conversation on social media	- You can easily connect with organisations, industries and people that suit your career pathway via e-networking sites, such as LinkedIn - You can find job opportunities directly from employers or employees through online networks - You can reach many potential targets - You can build connections beyond entry-level employment
	Disadvantages:
	- This may be deemed unprofessional - Prospective employers may trace your digital footprint and discover personal information that could affect your job opportunity - Your account may be subject to hacking personal information theft, and harassment from strangers

Exercise 7.1　Canvassing Template

Identify the method of cold canvassing you would like to adopt in job seeking.

Then, draft a template for this method that you could potentially use for your future job search. A sample template of a cold email is given here.

From: jason@amail.com
To: msjones@bmail.com
Subject: Editorial Internship Application

Dear Ms Jones,

My name is Jason Soh and I would like to apply for an editorial internship at ABC Publishing House. I am currently a double major in English and Media at the University of Australia, and I am looking to better my craft at your publishing house. I have loved ABC's books since I was young, with many of my childhood and current favourites being published by the house. Having over three years of editing and writing experience, I believe this internship would be an excellent opportunity to gain experience while making fundamental contributions to my favourite publisher.

During my study, I have learnt to write and edit various types of work, ranging from fiction to academic journals. I have also learnt to apply the Chicago Manual of Style guidelines to every piece I have written. I can communicate well with all types of people and can adapt to work in both individual and team settings. I am hardworking, determined and vigilant with details.

Besides this brief introduction, I have attached my résumé for further review. I would love to receive the opportunity to intern at ABC, and I believe I would be a valuable addition to your editorial team. Please get in touch with me via email if you have any enquiries. I appreciate your consideration, and I look forward to your response.

Sincerely,
Jason Soh

8 Innovative Strategies

Learning Objectives

1. Be aware of contemporary innovative strategies for gaining employment
2. Recognise tips to leverage your social network for job hunting

Innovative Strategies

1. Sometimes, it takes more than a great résumé to land a job—you may need a more innovative strategy.

2. For instance, instead of merely responding to job postings, you can create a social media presence to highlight your skills, abilities and talents for prospective employers. A solid social media presence should be seen as a complementary job-seeking strategy that can offer potential employers more insight into what you could offer.

3. Using social media can be challenging as you will be competing against a sea of applicants online. To stand out from the online crowd, you need to have the following:

   - A unique skill set
   - A polished video and digital portfolio
   - Interesting ways to boost your profile and presence
   - Patience!

Tips to Leverage Social Network for Job Hunting

1. Create your own professional website, blog or channel.

2. Keep your personal and professional identities separate.

3. Protect your personal security.

4. Be mindful of copyrighted content to avoid potential copyright infringement issues.

5. Edit and refine your portfolio, and upload the best one.

Exercise 8.1 Star Search

1. Find several videos online that demonstrate an innovative contemporary strategy for gaining employment.

2. Identify the skills, abilities or talent exhibited.

3. Identify job opportunities related to the video.

Video URL	Skill/ability/talent	Job opportunities

Exercise 8.2 Social Media Presentation

Select a job and prepare a social media presentation (i.e. YouTube video) to promote yourself to a potential employer of your choice.

Your social media presentation should be a maximum of three minutes in length and include the following:

1. An introduction of yourself and the job position you seek.

2. Your strengths.

3. The value or contributions you can bring to the company.

You can use the space below to draft your presentation.

_____

_____

_____

_____

_____

_____

_____

_____

_____

_____

_____

_____

_____

_____

_____

_____

_____

_____

9 Job Advertisement

Job Advertisement

1. A job advertisement is an announcement to inform you that a particular job position is available. It is one of the most common ways for employers to scout for potential employees. The advertisement could be done in various ways, such as via newspapers, social media, professional agencies or word of mouth.

2. Most job advertisements will contain the following information:
   - Job description
   - Job location
   - Qualification requirements
   - Selection criteria
   - Expression of interest requirements
   - Application process and deadline

Job Description

1. A job description gives an overview of the critical functions of a particular job.

2. It may specify details related to the job, such as the duties to perform, reporting line and salary range.

Job Location

1. A job location is a place where the job is performed.

2. While a job is generally performed in a specific location (workplace), some jobs require employees to travel to various locations or work remotely from any location.

Qualification Requirements

1. A job advertisement will specify the minimum school-entry related requirements. Below are some common examples:
   - Successful completion of Western Australian Certificate of Education
   - Meeting of the Australian Tertiary Admission Rank requirements for the institution and course offered
   - Completion of pre-requisite subjects with required scores
   - Demonstration of relevant work and extracurricular experiences

2. As part of the Australian Qualifications Framework, you can upgrade your qualification level to advance your career through the following ways:
   - School-based education
   - Work readiness programme
   - Apprenticeship and traineeship
   - Vocational Education and Training or VET
   - Technical and Further Education or TFE
   - Specialised training

Selection Criteria

1. Selection criteria are the attributes, skills and knowledge the employer specifies as essential for the job. These require you, as the applicant, to provide more information than what is contained in your résumé.

2. You must meet the selection criteria to be considered for the job. Employers use the criteria to better vet potential applicants by eliminating those not suited for the job.

3. Selection criteria are more commonly used for higher-level, career-focused positions. Examples of selection criteria include:
   - Ability to manage a diverse team
   - Exceptional leadership quality
   - Thorough understanding of current and future trends in the industry

Expression of Interest Requirements

1. Interest in a job can be expressed in a letter, through an e-application, on the phone, or face-to-face.

2. A job advertisement may also state that you register your interest in a position by registering with an employment agency or on the organisation's website.

3. A brief paragraph on your critical skills, qualifications and experience and an outline of why you are interested in the job position may also be required.

Application Process and Deadline

1. A job advertisement may require you to submit an application letter, cover letter and an expression of interest, along with a résumé.

2. Employers look at application letters to assess your suitability for the position. They also use the letter to look for your transferable skills.

3. Application processes differ between jobs, and higher-level positions usually go through a more stringent and competitive process. This can include a pre-employment assessment and a few rounds of interviews.

4. Application deadlines are determined by the employer and are usually stated in the job advertisement. As an applicant, you must meet the deadline requirement or risk losing the opportunity of securing the job.

Exercise 9.1 Ad Search

1. Find a job advertisement (online/print) by an organisation you wish to work in.

2. Identify the details available in the advertisement.

Exercise 9.2 Interpret the Ad

Based on the details available from the advertisement you found in the first exercise, interpret the following requirements:

1. Job description.

2. Job location.

3. Qualification requirements.

4. Selection criteria.

5. Expression of interest requirements.

6. Application process and deadline.

Job ad link	
Job position and title	
Job description	
Job location	

Qualification requirements	
Selection criteria	
Expression of interest requirements	
Application process and deadline	

10 Résumé Writing

Learning Objective

Refine your career portfolio

Résumé Writing

1. A résumé is often required by potential employers to ascertain whether you fit the position you applied for.

2. A résumé is a document detailing your professional experiences, education levels and skills relevant to the job you applied for. This document should be written in an easy-to-read, logical and concise way.

3. A résumé usually consists of the following details:

   - **Name**
     Birth name.

   - **Contact details**
     Address, phone number, email address.

   - **Working experiences**
     Name of organisation, role, duration of employment.

   - **Education level**
     Name of institution, certification, year of graduation.

   - **Skills**
     Linguistic, technical, professional (relevant to the job applied for).

   - **Hobbies and interests**
     Things you are passionate about besides work.

Exercise 10.1 Résumé Building

Visit https://www.kickresume.com/en and build your résumé using the templates given. You may refer to sample résumés available on the website.

11 Job Application

Learning Objective

Develop strategies to write a job application letter effectively

Job Application

1. Having decided to apply for a job advertised by a particular company or employer, the next step is to submit a job application. This indicates to the prospective employer that you are interested in the job.

2. All job applications must include the following:

   - **Reason for the application**
     State how you become aware of the job and clearly express your interest in it.

   - **Suitability for the job**
     Highlight your skills and experience that are relevant to the job.

   - **Contact details**
     Include your email address and phone number so that the employer can reach you.

Types of Application Letters

1. There are two types of application letters:

   - **Generic cold-call letter**
     Generic cold-call letters are sent out with résumés to enquire about the possibility of employment with an organisation that has not advertised any job vacancies.

     In the letter, express your interest in the organisation, identify your most relevant skills and experience, and explain what you could offer the organisation. The skills and interests described in the letter must match the job and organisation the letter is sent to.

- **Specific position application letter**
  This letter is written specifically in response to an advertised position. Your letter should highlight your most relevant qualifications and skills to increase your chances of landing an interview. A form letter (written from a template, rather than being specially composed for a specific recipient) is discouraged.

2. A brief cover letter should accompany a résumé, formal application letter, or online application. The cover letter introduces your qualifications, skills and personal interest in applying for the job. It should highlight your achievements and showcase your personality to distinguish you from other applicants.

3. A brief cover letter should be submitted via email when applying online.

Tips to Write an Application Letter

1. Show how your critical skills, competencies and experiences suit the job.

2. Ensure there are no grammar or spelling mistakes in your letter.

3. Use a professional tone and keep your sentences clear and short.

4. Have someone else proofread your letter.

Exercise 11.1 Job Application Letter

1. Based on the template given on the following page, write a job application letter for the position in the job advertisement you have searched for in **Exercise 9.1**.

2. Your letter must contain the following:
   - Reason for the application
   - Suitability for the job
   - Contact details

3. You may draft your letter on paper or electronically.

(insert own address)

(date)
Mr Jason Soh
Human Resources Manager
(insert name and address of the company)

Dear Mr Jason,
I am applying for the position of Copy Editor after noticing an online job advertisement for your company at www.jobsearch.com.

Reason for the application

I am currently a freelance copy editor and am ready to offer my enthusiasm, knowledge and experience to the dynamic publishing industry at a more professional level. During my time as an English and Media major student at the University of Australia, I became an intern at Australia University Publishing—the publishing company of the university—and gained my first practical publishing experience. I was introduced to and became familiar with standard publishing style guides such as the Chicago Manual of Style and learnt the basics of effective editing and fact-checking.

After graduating, I worked as an editorial assistant where I further gained invaluable insights into the industry and worked part-time as a receptionist at Success Tuition Centre. At the centre, I honed my communication and business-related skills with clients and the administration.

Suitability for the job

Beyond my editorial experience, I have a deep passion for English culture and the language. I was a youth ambassador to the United Kingdom through a cultural exchange programme, and I have been consuming all forms of literary work for as long as I can remember. My passion for reading and writing will ensure my commitment to my work.

The written word has shaped my life, and I would be thrilled to receive the opportunity to work at (name of company). I am hardworking, open to new experiences, and ready to face and tackle challenges that I may encounter at the company.

If you need more information, I can be reached at 0123456789 or jamessmith@amail.com.

Contact details

Yours sincerely,
James Smith

12 Job Interview

Learning Objective

Identify strategies to participate in job interviews successfully, such as recognising:

- Types of job interviews
- Common interview questions
- The SAO method

Types of Job Interviews

1. Once an employer receives a job application from you, they will typically organise an interview. This is a way to vet all applicants before deciding on those deemed fit for the job. While this step may be done out of formality, it is a good platform for employers to learn more about you and other job applicants before recruiting.

2. There are three common types of interviews, depending on the job you are going for:

   - **One-on-one interviews**
   This type of interview usually refers to an interview by the person who will employ you, such as the boss, business owner, or human resource manager.

   This is a standard interview and can be done face-to-face or via phone and online platforms (Skype, Zoom, etc.). The interviewer will direct the conversation at the start, and you will have the opportunity to ask questions towards the end.

   - **Panel interviews**
   This type of interview is usually for higher-level positions with larger organisations or the government. It will usually involve three to four interview panellists, typically representing different departments. Each panel member has the opportunity to ask you about your experience and goals.

   - **Group interviews**
   This type of interview is where you and other candidates are interviewed together. It may be conducted by a single interviewer or a panel of interviewers. Group interviews may be used when a new enterprise is starting or expanding and is looking for a way to effectively and quickly manage a lot of applicants. This method is part of a bulk "cattle call" (similar to an audition process).

Tips to Ace Job Interviews

How do you make a great impression at an interview? Here are some interview tips for an effective interview:

1. **Be prepared**
   - Find out about the organisation (its business, products, history, competitors, etc.)
   - Find out the details of the interview session (interview location, duration to reach the interview location, transportation issues, contact person, etc.)
   - Have extra copies of your résumé and references, in case required
   - Anticipate and prepare for common interview questions
   - Make a list of questions for the interviewer

2. **Be presentable**
   - Dress suitably and professionally
   - Minimise accessories; only wear what is necessary
   - Ensure good personal hygiene

3. **Be personable**
   - Greet people warmly and use the appropriate salutation
   - Look into the interviewer's eyes when conversing
   - Nod your head to greet or agree appropriately
   - Sit upright and do not fidget!

4. **Sell yourself confidently**
   - Clearly articulate your responses
   - Highlight your strengths with specific examples
   - Be confident and enthusiastic in your responses
   - Ask if you need clarification

5. **Reflect on your experience**
   - Thank the interviewer for their time
   - Send a thank you email after the interview
   - Be patient in waiting for the results
   - Contact the organisation to follow up if you have not heard any news for a while
   - Do not give up if you are rejected. Try again!

Common Interview Questions

1. Prepare the answers to questions you will most likely be asked to avoid fumbling during the interview.

2. Some common questions include the following:
   - Tell me about yourself
   - Why do you want this job?
   - Why should we hire you?
   - How can you contribute to this organisation?
   - What are your strengths?
   - What are your areas for improvement?
   - Do you have any questions?

The SAO Method

1. The SAO method of Situation/Action/Outcome is a simple technique you can use to prepare for job interviews.

2. The following details the SAO method:
   - **Situation**
     Describe a task or situation where you demonstrated transferable skills or work-related competencies.
   - **Action**
     Give examples of what you achieved and how you achieved it. Identify the resources used, such as workforce, equipment, etc.
   - **Outcome**
     Summarise the outcome (Was it successful? Why? If unsuccessful, how could you improve?).

> **Q: What do you consider as your main strength?**
>
> **A:** I would consider leadership as my main strength. I was given the opportunity to lead the debate club as president at school. I was in charge of recruiting and training debaters for competition, using my experience as a seasoned debater. As a result of leading the club during that period, my team was able to win the national debate competition.

Source: Adapted from Southam (n.d.)

Figure 12.1   A sample interview Q&A using the SAO method

Exercise 12.1 Mock Interview

Select a job and prepare for an interview with a potential employer in an industry of your choice.

Some sample interview questions can be found below for your preparation:

Can you tell me about yourself?	What are your goals?	What are your strengths and weaknesses?	Why did you choose this company?
Why did you choose this job?	Who is your career mentor?	Where do you see yourself in 5–10 years?	Why should we hire you?
What are your learning takeaways from your experiences?	Can you tell us about your work/ volunteering experience?	What do you know about this company?	What strategies do you have to overcome your weaknesses?

13 Equity in the Workplace

1. Realise the need to recognise and adjust to diversity within a workplace, encompassing differences in:
   - Age
   - Ethnicity
   - Physical ability
2. Understand factors that create effective workplaces, including the policy of Equal Employment Opportunity
3. Be aware of affirmative action plans or regulations of a particular country

Equity

1. Equity refers to the fair treatment of others.
2. **Workplace diversity**, **equal employment opportunity** and **affirmative action** are three components of equity in the workplace.

Workplace Diversity

1. Diversity is increasingly becoming the norm in workplaces in today's globalised world. You will need to be able to interact with people of varied ages, abilities, backgrounds and cultures.
2. Workplace diversity can be an asset, as it enhances work-related outcomes due to the workforce's broader perspectives, experiences and creeds.
3. There is a need to recognise and adjust to diversity within a workplace if the workforce comprises a wide range of people of different ages, ethnicities and abilities.
   - **Diversity: Age**
     When dealing with people from different age groups:
     - Consider whether a person is likely to understand terminologies and descriptions they may not be familiar with
     - Be aware of etiquette issues when dealing with older people (e.g. formalities, manners, slang)
     - Be mindful of legal issues when dealing with minors

- **Diversity: Ethnicity**

  When dealing with people from different ethnic groups:

  - Learn basic-level greetings and instructions in other languages
  - Commit to understanding and celebrating a diverse range of histories, cultures, traditions as well as languages
  - Broaden your understanding of cultural communication issues and cultural sensitivities

- **Diversity: Ability**

  Contemporary workplaces are inclusive of people with different and varied abilities, and there might be people with the following disabilities:

  - Physical impairment (e.g. blind, deaf)
  - Intellectual impairment (e.g. dyslexia, Down syndrome)
  - Emotional impairment (e.g. depression, bipolar)

  When dealing with people with different abilities:

  - Develop empathy and be more understanding of a person's situation
  - If necessary, ask for any modifications or changes that might be needed to enable the person to do their job effectively

Equal Employment Opportunity

1. Equal Employment Opportunity (EEO) is the policy of offering everyone the same opportunities for employment and promotion without discrimination. It aims to provide a level playing field, which is an underlying notion of equity.

2. An example of equal opportunity legislation in Australia is the 1984 Equal Opportunity Act (WA). The Act was enacted to deal with discrimination and harassment and to promote equality regardless of the social-economic status of the citizens.

3. The Equal Opportunity Commission is the state body that deals with equal opportunity and discrimination issues.

Affirmative Action

1. Affirmative action refers to policies and practices of a government or organisation targeting groups that are under-represented in an organisation, industry or society at large.

2. Under-representation is often caused by socio-demographic factors (including age, ethnicity and ability).

3. Affirmative action can help foster inclusivity in areas such as:

   - New hire and promotion policies
   - Grant disbursements and incentives
   - Education and training opportunities

TAKE A QUIZ!

Take a diversity test to see if you do indeed appreciate diversity.
Test link: https://implicit.harvard.edu/implicit/takeatest.html

Exercise 13.1 Diversity

1. In groups of three or four, discuss other areas of diversity in the workplace that could potentially be subject to discrimination.

2. What kind of discriminatory practices could occur in the areas of diversity listed in the table below?

Area of diversity	Discriminatory practices
Age	
Ethnicity	
Ability	

Research 13.1 Equal Employment Opportunity

Research the 1984 Equal Opportunity Act (WA).

Choose one form of discrimination outlined in the Act, and present your findings in class.

Research 13.2 Affirmative Action

Research affirmative action plans that the government of a particular country has implemented for the society.

Present your findings in class. You can use the space below to draft your findings.

_____

_____

_____

_____

_____

_____

_____

_____

_____

_____

_____

_____

_____

_____

_____

14 Respect in Communication

Respect in Communication

1. Good communicators are mindful of the **values**, **beliefs** and **cultural expectations** held by others.

2. They will take care not to offend people by infringing on these differences.

Values

1. A value is a personal feeling or ideal which influences your ethics and actions. Values are things you deem necessary (e.g. I value equal opportunities for either gender).

2. A social or societal value is an ideal shared by a group of like-minded stakeholders, such as employees, shareholders, unions, and people groups.

Beliefs

1. A belief refers to a set of thoughts or reasons that influences your way of thinking (e.g. I believe there should not be a difference in the treatment of either gender).

2. Beliefs grow from what you experience and think about. Everyone has a right to their own beliefs.

Cultural Expectations

1. Cultural expectations refer to shared expectations of a particular group about the proper behaviour in different situations. For instance, it is considered rude and disrespectful to point to a person with your index finger in some cultures.

2. Cultural expectations are usually embedded over time and are closely related to societal values.

3. Misunderstandings surrounding cultural expectations can occur due to generalisations and ignorance of potential differences.

Exercise 14.1 Values and Beliefs

Identify three differences between values and beliefs.

Values	Beliefs

Exercise 14.2 Cultural Expectations: Think—Pair—Share

1. List three cultural expectations you know/observe/discover from research.
2. Which of those cultural expectations do you strongly relate to or agree with?
3. Which of those cultural expectations do you disagree with or cannot relate to?
4. Why do you think such cultural expectations exist in those contexts?

Cultural expectation	Can you relate to it? Do you agree/disagree with it?	Why does the expectation exist?

15 Cross-Cultural Communication

Intercultural Understanding

1. Intercultural understanding comes from a mutual exchange of ideas and norms between different communities. It also stems from a deep respect for all cultures.

2. You develop intercultural understanding as you learn to do the following:

   - Value your own culture, language and beliefs
   - Develop awareness of the values, languages and customs of other cultural groups—such as the Asian, Aboriginal, or Torres Strait Islander peoples—and their place in contemporary society and culture

3. This understanding involves recognising commonalities and differences between cultures in different countries and within individual workplaces through **cross-cultural communication**.

Cross-Cultural Communication

1. In cross-cultural communication, differences between cultures are recognised and understood.

2. Some critical questions to ask when communicating with people from across cultures include:

   - To whom are you communicating?
   - What should you do, or not do, when communicating?
   - What issues do you need to consider?

3. Besides being mindful of cross-cultural communication in your personal and professional life, you must also consider the "**new normal**" **of communication** following restrictions imposed to contain the COVID-19 pandemic.

"New Normal" of Communication

1. The COVID-19 pandemic has significantly altered the way of communicating. Once deemed acceptable behaviour, certain practices no longer work given the circumstances.

2. Driven by health and safety concerns and strict regulations by the authorities, the following are now considered the "new normal":

   • Wearing a face mask when you are around others

   • Sanitising or washing your hands regularly

   • Physically distancing yourself from others

Exercise 15.1 Do's and Don'ts

1. Look at the given table below. Describe when, and when not, to do each of the following in different cross-cultural work-related situations.

2. If possible, analyse another issue or action which may occur in cross-cultural communication.

Issue/Action	When to do it	When not to do it
Using honorifics when addressing someone		
Questioning a directive		

Issue/Action	When to do it	When not to do it
Communicating by email		
Shaking hands		
Giving gifts		

Issue/Action	When to do it	When not to do it
Bowing your head		
Making eye contact		
Being in close physical proximity with others		

16 Global Trends

Globalisation

1. Countries engage in global trade by exporting and importing goods and services. The commercial world extends across international boundaries, and Australia is a critical player in worldwide import and export markets such as metals and mining. The global workplace consists of multinational companies looking to increase their international competitiveness.

2. Globalisation will influence workplace requirements and individual career development. The five main trends that affect the global workforce are the **ageing workforce**, **mobile population**, **changing work roles of family members**, **e-commerce** and **overseas outsourcing**.

Ageing Workforce

1. Australia has an ageing population, which indicates that the workforce's average age is rising.

2. This is due to better standards of living and healthcare, which increase life expectancies. In addition, families also have fewer children due to higher living costs.

Table 16.1   Challenges and opportunities of an ageing population

Challenges	Opportunities
• Fewer young workers to replace retiring workers • Fewer workers paying income tax • A loss of specialised skills and experience, or shortage of skills • Changes in social support needs • High welfare costs • Shortages in community infrastructure (e.g. healthcare)	• Opportunities to work longer • Opportunities to engage in mentoring and skills transfer • Growth in healthcare, tourism and recreation industries • An increase in community engagement

Mobile Population

1. Most employment opportunities in Australia are centralised in major cities and regional centres.

2. As major metropolitan areas become larger, people need to relocate to areas where they can access employment opportunities or commute long distances to work (e.g. Fly-in/Fly-out and Drive-in/Drive-out where workers living in remote areas have to fly or drive to work).

3. Labour mobility commonly occurs in seasonal industries (e.g. agriculture, forestry, tourism).

Table 16.2   Challenges and opportunities of a mobile population

Challenges	Opportunities
• An increase in price for inner and middle suburban houses • A cease in operations of significant employers in regional areas • Forced relocation of workers and families to areas with more job opportunities • Shortages in workers in regional, remote and rural areas	• Cheaper prices for outer-urban houses, attracting high-income holidaymakers and retirees • An increase in employment rates • Improved transportation and mobility access • More opportunities to travel for work

Changing Work Roles of Family Members

1. Parents are now more engaged in the workforce, and the demographic characteristics of a family have evolved.

2. Today, shared parenting, dual income, and work-life balance are seen as essential for improving the well-being of society and standards of living.

3. Some of the demographic characteristics of an Australian family include:
   - Smaller families
   - Increased number of single-parent families
   - Increased number of working mothers
   - Increased number of parents working more than one job

E-Commerce

1. E-commerce refers to commercial transactions that use electronic data transmission mechanisms.

2. Standard e-commerce business models include **B2B**, **B2C**, **C2C** and **C2B**.

Table 16.3   Types of e-commerce business models

Type	Opportunities
B2B	Businesses manage supply chains using online transactions
B2C	Consumers engage in online retail or pay bills
C2C	Consumers transact with each other (e.g. classified advertisements, auctions)
C2B	Consumers form a buying group (co-operative) to negotiate with businesses

Overseas Outsourcing

1. Outsourcing refers to the use of contracted service providers to render non-core services for an organisation, allowing the organisation to focus its efforts on its core competencies.

2. In a global economy, many organisations increasingly rely on overseas outsourcing to be more internationally competitive.

3. Many organisations outsource products or services they no longer produce or provide themselves.

4. Types of overseas outsourcing include:

- Sourcing components, inputs, supplies or equipment from overseas suppliers
- Manufacturing some or all production outputs from overseas sources
- Relocating some operations to overseas locations
- Bringing in skilled labour from overseas
- Using data processing and customer service provided by overseas firms
- Contracting specialised experts and consultants from overseas
- Sharing skills, knowledge and expertise with global partners

Table 16.4   Advantages and disadvantages of overseas outsourcing

Advantages	Disadvantages
<ul><li>Less cost incurred for outsourcing than hiring local employees</li><li>A saving in costs for employers</li><li>Better focus to perform core tasks, as outsourcing focuses on non-core tasks (e.g. customer service)</li></ul>	<ul><li>Less direct supervision over outsourced workers/contractors</li><li>Lower product or service quality due to less direct supervision</li><li>Retrenchment of local workers</li></ul>

Investigation 16.1 Report Writing

Investigate and produce a written report on the following:

1. Discuss a global trend in the Australian workforce based on a particular industry. Refer to the table below for the types of industry available in Australia.

2. Investigate and provide information about two possible impacts of the global trend on a particular industry chosen in the previous question.

Types of Industries in Australia	
1. Agriculture, forestry and fishing	12. Rental, hiring and real estate services
2. Mining	13. Professional, scientific, and technical services
3. Manufacturing	14. Administrative and support services
4. Electricity, gas, water and waste services	15. Public administration and safety
5. Construction	16. Education and training
6. Wholesale trade	17. Health care and social assistance
7. Retail trade	18. Arts and recreation services
8. Accommodation and food services	19. Other services, including personal services (like laundry, hairdressers and day spas), funeral and religious services, car repair and maintenance (like spray painting), and other mechanical repair services.
9. Transport, postal and warehousing	
10. Information media and telecommunications	
11. Financial and insurance services	

Source: Adapted from Job Outlook (n.d.)

17 | Risk Management

Risk Management

1. Career management involves managing risks, also known as opportunity costs. Opportunity cost is the next best alternative that has to be forgone when making choices in decision-making.

2. The types of risks involved in career decision-making might change depending on where you are in the stage of your career life cycle.

Table 17.1 Risks in career decisions

Stage of career life cycle	Risks
Entry	Employment, readjustment, retention
Growth	Training, career progression, opportunities, job prospects
Consolidator	Fulfilment, work/life balance, development
Change	Skills, re-training, family roles, values and belief

Personal Risks

1. At times, you may have to manage personal risks to advance your career. At other times, you manage these risks to increase job satisfaction and fulfilment, which people say money cannot buy.

2. Some personal risks include **relocating**, **accepting less pay**, and **taking a gap year**.

    - **Relocating**

        – You may have to move to a different geographical region to pursue job opportunities. This usually occurs at the start of a career, with you taking on opportunities away from your home.

        – Relocating sometimes occurs due to structural factors; for instance, specific skills are not needed locally, or jobs of a particular industry are not available in nearby areas

Table 17.2   Benefits and risks of relocating for a job

Benefits	Risks
• You become proactive and go to where the jobs are • You learn to be independent, which is a transferable skill • You have access to better job opportunities • You expand your social as well as professional network • You learn new cultures and different ways of doing things	• You may suffer from loneliness and homesickness • You have to support yourself living independently • You will be apart from family and close friends • You have to acclimatise yourself to a new environment and community • You may not be working a secure or long-term job

    - **Accepting less pay**

        – You may be presented with a job opportunity that pays less but offers greater long-term benefits either professionally or personally

        – This situation may occur when you are still new in the industry or taking on an apprenticeship. Sometimes, accepting less pay is part of career growth as you take a new role in a different industry or occupation.

Table 17.3   Benefits and risks of accepting less pay

Benefits	Risks
• You enjoy more pathway opportunities • You enjoy work-life balance, if you take a less demanding and thus lower-paying job • You gain new skills and knowledge, if you take a role in a different industry • You broaden your professional network, if you take a role in a different industry	• You may be financially unstable • You may not enjoy adequate standards of living • You may not be able to leverage the opportunities presented in the new industry • You may lower your job security, if you are restarting a career

- **Taking a gap year**
  - If you take a break and defer your studies, you can take the opportunity to pursue other interests, such as travelling, building life skills, developing transferable skills and even gaining industry experience
  - If you have had a career, you can use a gap year to take a career break to reassess and develop new transferable skills

Table 17.4 Benefits and risks of taking a gap year

Benefits	Risks
• You build life experiences • You develop transferable or specific skills • You contribute to the community • You reassess and clarify career goals • You enable a change in career direction	• You may lose your career momentum • You may feel unaccomplished if nothing significant is achieved • You may find it challenging to get back into a study/work routine • You may be left in debt • You may lose direction if the gap year is prolonged

Unexpected Events

1. The workplace can be a volatile environment, and you may encounter unforeseen incidents that you will need to deal with.

2. The following are some examples of unexpected events that may occur in a work-related situation:
   - No stock
   - Workplace accidents
   - Resource constraints
   - Equipment breakdowns

3. Be prepared to do the following to manage unexpected events effectively:
   - Have contingency plans
   - Outline clear standard operating procedures
   - Communicate with/report to the immediate supervisor/manager/employer
   - Be adequately trained to deal with such occurrences (a preventive measure)

Reflection 17.1 Personal Risk Identification

1. What personal risk(s) do you think you will face or have faced?

2. How do you ensure that the risk(s) are managed in a way that strengthens your career goals?

Exercise 17.1 Unexpected Event Identification

1. In your group, identify an unexpected event that could take place in work-related situations. Be as detailed as possible!

2. Provide clear strategies to deal with such an event in the workplace.

3. How could the incident be prevented in the future?

Unexpected event	
Strategies to prevent the unexpected event	

How to prevent in the future?

18 Training and Retraining

Training

1. Effective training is crucial to developing a skilled and knowledgeable labour force. Employees at all levels of an organisation must be competent in performing their work roles and tasks.

2. When you are trained as an employee, you will exhibit effective work skills that will help improve the company's work quality, resulting in greater customer satisfaction. You can consider **training** and **retraining** to be part of your career development. This will enhance your prospects for promotion and career progression.

3. You may sometimes need to seek advice, feedback and support from your immediate supervisor or manager about the types of training you should undergo to improve yourself as an employee. This is important as your superior will provide an expert opinion on your current performance, and suggest appropriate measures to increase your career enhancement opportunities through training and retraining.

Types of Training

1. **Formal training**
   - This type of training leads to certification and qualifications
   - Examples include school certificates and university qualifications

2. **Informal training**
   - Learning comes from working on the job and from experiences at the workplace
   - This type of training includes supervision, day-to-day assistance, mentoring, coaching, demonstration, advice and support

3. **Off-the-job training**
   - This refers to training in a formal learning environment rather than in the "everyday" workplace
   - This type of training often leads to certification

4. **On-the-job training**
   - This can be formal or informal training that takes place directly at the workplace
   - This type of training is usually a normal part of workplace learning

5. **Professional development**
   - This refers to training opportunities, usually funded by employers, offered to help you upskill and develop your career

6. **Competency-based training**
   - Learning is based on demonstrating achievement of learning outcomes by performing specific tasks
   - For instance, Australian Apprenticeship—an apprenticeship incentive programme by the Australian government—offers opportunities for you to train, study and earn an income in many occupations and trades

Retraining

1. Retraining occurs when you develop new skills through formal training or enhance your competencies by broadening your skills set. Retraining can involve acquiring skills and qualifications to support a career shift or relaunch.

2. You can become deskilled through advances in technology. But new career opportunities can emerge during a career life cycle, and retraining can enable you to upskill and take advantage of emerging opportunities.

3. Structural economic shifts that can undermine job security can also open up new opportunities.

Exercise 18.1 Training You Need

1. Pick and list three occupations you are interested in or curious about.

2. Identify two examples of further education/training that you require for each of the occupations listed above.

Exercise 18.2 Milestones

1. Draw a pathway timeline that maps out your life.

2. On the timeline, show significant milestones you hope to achieve and the ages you plan to achieve them. Include personal and social milestones.

3. On top of your milestones, show any education or training you think you will need to achieve them.

Research 18.1 Retraining

Discuss the following:

1. What could be some potential benefits of retraining?

2. What risks must you manage if you are considering retraining?

_____

_____

_____

_____

_____

_____

_____

_____

_____

_____

_____

_____

_____

_____

19 E-Networking

Learning Objective

Identify strategies to remain employable in constantly changing workplaces through e-networking

E-Networking Strategies

1. **Formal online networking**

   Professional e-networking platforms such as LinkedIn and Twitter are more suited for professional networking rather than for seeking entry-level jobs. You can, however, connect or "link" to organisations and industries that suit your career pathway and follow influential people in the industry who can be important networking contacts.

   However, you must remember the following:

   - Manage your privacy settings. Your boss could check your profile!
   - Check if the person or business contacting you is reliable, reputable and safe
   - Be mindful that if an opportunity sounds too good to be true, it could be a scam

2. **Informal online networking**

   Industry colleagues may create informal online communities and networks based on shared interests or philosophies. Owners of these communities and networks might use the platform to share their views or offer advice, while you as a jobseeker might find the platform helpful to seek job openings.

   However, you must remember the following:

   - Keep your professional and personal social media accounts separate
   - Keep your professional and personal emails separate

3. **Online showcasing**

   If you follow an artistic, creative, performative or craft-based pathway (such as digital media, video, film, music, performance, art, or design), you can display samples of your work online. An online portfolio of your work can help enhance your reputation, showcase your skills and broaden your profile.

   However, you must remember the following:

   - Ensure your communication online is professional
   - Monitor comments made by friends to ensure their communication is professional

Tips to Ace E-Networking

1. **Be professional**
   - Maintain a responsible digital footprint. Keep personal posts to your private network. You are likely to be e-searched by a potential employer
   - Make sure the information you send to others is in a format that can be accessed
   - Be aware of standard business hours

2. **Be safe online**
   - Ensure the organisations you are interested in are real, and if the person you are corresponding with is who they say they are
   - Avoid sharing unnecessary personal information
   - Avoid posting or mass-sharing your CV
   - Refrain from providing your photograph unless you can ascertain the receiver's reliability and that your photograph will be kept private

Research 19.1 E-Networking

Discuss the following:

1. Which is more effective in spreading and gaining new information—sharing with one of your best friends or sharing with an acquaintance from class?

2. How can you increase the range and diversity of people you talk to? Specify three concrete ways.

3. How can technology help you in networking?

You can use the space below to draft your points.

_____

_____

_____

_____

_____

_____

_____

_____

_____

_____

20 Decision-Making

Learn strategies to assist you in making decisions using the PADS decision-making process

Decision-Making

1. One way to make yourself a better decision-maker is to use a step-by-step approach to guide your thought process on setting and achieving your goals.

2. A decision-making process such as **PADS** will help you deal with how to reach important decisions or resolutions.

PADS

1. PADS is a series of steps to guide you on how to go about making a decision or reaching a solution.

2. As it helps you deal with potential problems, PADS also acts as an ongoing problem-solving tool.

Source: Adapted from Carolan (2016)

Figure 20.1 Effective problem-solving and decision-making using PADS

Reflection 20.1 Life Decisions

1. Think back to the end of your high school life. Would you have made any decisions differently if you had the opportunity to do so right now?

2. What are some significant decisions you have to make in your life right now?

3. How can you ensure you make the best decision for yourself?

Investigation 20.1 PADS Application

Using the PADS decision-making process, solve a current problem you have.

Identify the **P**roblem	
Investigate **A**lternatives	

Make a **D**ecision

Evaluate the **S**olution

21 Work-Life Balance

Work-Life Balance

1. Effective time management is vital to achieving a work-life balance between career demands and personal life. Personal and family responsibilities are likely to influence career pathway choices.

2. As the nature of work becomes more demanding and complex, managing different aspects of life—such as family and personal and professional responsibilities—becomes a daily challenge. Balancing work and life is essential for the well-being of society, as it is the key to improving standards of living.

3. Some key workplace trends that challenge work-life balance include:

   • Increased demands and work expectations from employers

   • Long commutes due to work being farther away

   • Remote work arrangements that make work and personal commitments inseparable

   • Longer work hours or overtime

   • Both parents with children have multiple jobs

Work-Life Balance Strategies

1. Due to increased awareness of the importance of work-life balance, there is a growing demand for flexible work arrangements.

2. Some examples of flexible work arrangements adopted by many organisations are as follows:

   • **Casual work arrangements**

     – Employment is on a non-permanent basis

     – Employment can be terminated at short notice

    – Employer is not required to supply leave and other entitlements

    – A higher hourly rate of pay is usually offered

- **Part-time work**
  - Employment carries a time fraction that is less than a full-time job
  - You are entitled to all privileges enjoyed by full-time workers but on a pro-rata basis
  - The part-time work is usually permanent (working regular hours but fewer hours a week than full-time workers)

- **Job sharing**
  - A job is divided between more than one worker
  - You and another worker may work on the same days in the week to allow continuity and avoid duplication of tasks

- **Multi-skilling**
  - You are trained in a variety of skills that are highly demanded
  - You and other workers can be rotated through different work tasks
  - Work can be shared during busy schedules since you and other workers have been trained to be competent in various tasks

- **Redeployment**
  - You can be redeployed or moved from one job task within an organisation to another
  - This may be desirable due to changes in technology, upskilling of staff, or part of the multi-skilling process

- **Hot desking**
  - This involves you and other workers using a shared or temporary workspace, work station or office during different periods
  - The use of resources can be optimised
  - Hot desking is a cost-effective arrangement for work settings with dynamic workers who may not need a full-time office

- **Outsourcing**
  - External stakeholders undertake work for a specified period or a particular service or job function
  - Employers outsource specialised skills when needed (e.g. ICT, marketing, security, event management, cleaning, transport)

- **Flexitime**
  - A flexitime work schedule allows you to choose your workday start and finish times
  - If you put in additional hours at the request of an employer, you can take the same amount of time off at a later date

- **Telecommunicating**
  - Also called remote working, telecommunicating is an arrangement that allows you to work away from the company's offices
  - You can work from home using various telecommunication technologies, such as video conferencing, email, telephone, and shared online platforms

Class Activity 21.1 Schedule

1. Draw a clock or timeline and determine your daily activities or tasks for today. Compare your schedule with the person next to you.

2. Draw a clock or timeline and determine your weekly activities or tasks for this week. Compare your schedule with the person next to you and give each other input on whether you think your partner has a work-life balance.

Research 21.1 Work vs Life

Discuss some of the causes of work-life imbalance. Refer to the table below to help with your discussion.

Causes of work-life imbalance

- Longer work hours
- Inflexible work hours
- Unpaid overtime
- Higher-level job
- Higher job expectations
- Multiple jobs
- Technology

- Cost-of-living pressures
- Mortgage stress
- High parenting costs
- Childcare issues
- Increased commute time
- Fly-in/Fly-out and Drive-in/Drive-out
- Work-related travel

Research 21.2 Flexible Work Arrangements

Discuss the following:

1. Choose two flexible work arrangements. Explain how the work arrangements could assist, yet also threaten, work-life balance.

2. What are some other flexible work arrangements you are aware of?

Reflection 21.1 Future Planning

1. List down all the main activities in your current phase of life.

2. List down all the main activities which will be essential in five years.

3. How important do you think work-life balance is to you in your future career?

4. What kind of work arrangement will you prefer in your future career?

_____

_____

_____

_____

_____

_____

_____

_____

_____

_____

_____

_____

_____

_____

_____

_____

_____

_____

22 Employment Opportunities

Consider labour market information to identify employment opportunities, including:
- Self-employment
- Product development

Self-Employment

1. Self-employment means to work for yourself as a freelancer or as the sole owner of a business. It may be a great career option if you want to pursue a specific career path or if you have a desire to sell your skills or expertise.

2. Understanding labour market data would help identify self-employment and business opportunities. Examples of such information include:

   - **Demographics**
     The traits of a population include size, growth rate, average age, and level of education.

   - **New technology**
     Innovations that help organisations work smarter and faster, leading to improved products, processes, and services.

   - **Key occupational needs and requirements**
     Jobs that are in demand and the skills you need to do those jobs.

   - **Local, provincial, and national economic situations**
     These shape the ups and downs of the labour market, including the strength of specific regions and changes in employment rates.

   - **Industry activity**
     The change in growth and job outlook in major industries.

   - **Labour market trends**
     The combined effects of all the influences in this list.

Why Choose Self-Employment?

1. Self-employment involves a high level of commitment. There are some myths surrounding self-employment that may or may not be necessarily true:
   - You get to do what you love
   - You can be your own boss
   - You have a lot of freedom (e.g. choosing what you want to work on, setting your own work hours, etc.)
   - You will not have job security
   - You mainly work alone and may not have a solid social network
   - You have to do everything yourself without support

2. Regardless, you can consider self-employment for the following reasons:
   - You want flexibility in your schedule
   - You want more control over your ideas, projects and the work that you do
   - You do not work well with others
   - You are comfortable being "the decider"
   - You have a robust support system—family and friends who support your venture

Product Development

1. Product development is the creation of products with new or different characteristics that offer new or additional benefits to the customer. It may involve modifying an existing product or its presentation or formulating an entirely new product that satisfies a newly defined demand or market niche.

2. Product development involves time, money, skills and a high level of risk.

3. Some examples of product development outcomes include:
   - Smartphones
   - Touch screens and tablets
   - Hybrid cars
   - E-books

Stages of Product Development

1. **Product ideas**
   Research existing customers, target markets, technology and competitors. Use this information to identify an opportunity for a niche market or an unmet customer need, or a way to use value and quality to capture market share. Ask people in the industry for product ideas and survey customers for feedback on existing products.

2. **Idea evaluation**

Make a list of possible product ideas and evaluate them with business leaders or a product development team. It is good to consider ideas with people from various business functions, such as marketing, production, finance, and sales. Each idea can then be evaluated more thoroughly, based on whether the product has marketing potential, whether the business can produce it efficiently, if there is time and money to produce it, and if staff can sell it. Look at the expected sales, costs, and profit for each idea. Discuss the pros and cons and select the best idea.

3. **Product concept evaluation**

Add details to the idea, such as potential target markets, designs, colours, and names. Seek feedback from customers and people in the industry about the idea. Run focus groups to gather feedback about the idea, possible product names and advertising strategy. Analyse the market to identify competitors selling or developing similar products and substitutes.

4. **Prototype testing**

Develop the idea into a prototype once the best idea is chosen and tested. Analyse, test the product and provide and gather feedback. You can use positive feedback for advertising and promotions, and negative feedback can be addressed by improving the prototype.

5. **Market testing**

Conduct market testing when the prototype is refined. A small number of samples can be manufactured and distributed to customers. Market testing is often part of the campaign to spark interest in the product before its full launch.

6. **Product launch**

Prepare for customer orders and retail distribution. Use a range of promotional strategies to generate interest and demand for the product. New products may need a more comprehensive marketing plan because customers need to be educated about a new, unfamiliar product and its benefits.

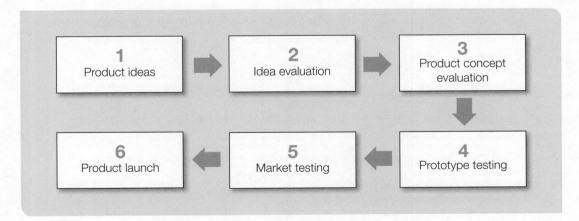

Figure 22.1 Six stages of the new product development process

Class Activity 22.1 Business Idea

1. Consider which industries you may be interested in if you were self-employed.

2. Identify new opportunities in those industries.

3. Come up with a business idea.

4. If your idea is related to product development, apply the stages of product development in your plan—it will be interesting to see a prototype!

Industry	
Opportunities	

Business idea	

23 Being Enterprising

Learning Objective

Understand the importance of being enterprising in a global economy, including:

- Making international business links
- Identifying consumer gaps and niche markets
- Using technology

International Business Links

1. Globalisation and technology present both pressures and opportunities for change. Large organisations build international business links through outsourcing and strategic partnerships.

2. International business links will result in the expansion of global commerce, creating opportunities for firms to be outward-looking and risk-taking.

3. As a future employee, take the following proactive steps:
   - Improve your cross-communication skills
   - Develop functional language skills related to key market areas
   - Learn the basics of international trade, including exporting, importing and the impact of exchange rates on transactions
   - Develop an online presence
   - Consider starting an online niche enterprise

Consumer Gaps and Niche Markets

1. The Internet and social media networks have enabled us to identify and service consumer gaps in the market, namely places or products that current businesses are not serving.

2. Large organisations operate using economies of scale, and many find servicing small limited markets to be cost-ineffective. So, small and micro-niche providers have entered the marketplace to service these gaps.

3. The following are some examples of niche products and services that can fulfil consumer gaps:
   - Organic produce
   - Fair-trade coffee
   - Specialised dance studios
   - 3-D-printed jewellery
   - Web designer specialising in retail platforms for small businesses

Technology

1. Technology can assist businesses to get their products to international customers. Businesses can have customers shop directly on their websites from anywhere in the world, instead of having a network of retail stores to sell their products.

2. Technology also allows businesses to communicate directly with customers globally to provide assistance or improve their services.

Homework 23.1 Business Research

Based on your business idea in the **Employment Opportunities** chapter, fill out the following table:

International business links *Research a website or online platform that can help you reach a broad online audience.*	e.g.: • Amazon • Instagram

Consumer gap and niche markets *Identify the consumer gaps and niche markets for your business.*	e.g.: Consumer gap • The older generation may not be interested in illustrated art products such as stickers, badges and pins Niche market: • Art students, artists and collectors
Technology *Describe the technological hardware/ software required for your venture.*	e.g.: • Drawing tablet/iPad to illustrate designs • Sticker printer to print out stickers • Sewing machine to make patches

24 Resource Management

Resource Management

1. Resource management refers to maximising productivity in the use of input to generate the most efficient mix of output.

2. It focuses on **managing human**, **physical**, **financial** and **technological resources**, as outlined in Figure 24.1.

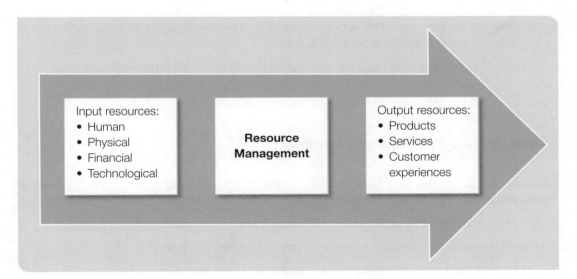

Figure 24.1 Resource management is the process by which a business manages its resources effectively and efficiently

Managing Human Resources

1. People are considered the most critical resource in any organisation.

2. Human resource management is essential to ensure the business remains competitive and desirable to current and potential employees.

Managing Physical Resources

1. Physical resources are all the materials that produce a good or service. Examples include raw materials, components, stock and consumables.

2. Physical resources are usually variable costs that fluctuate directly with the units produced. Therefore, economies of scale will enable businesses to save on these costs.

Managing Financial Resources

1. Budget is an essential financial management planning tool. It lists forecasted revenue and expenses.

2. Comparing forecasts with actual amounts will enable corrective actions on issues that need investigation, especially if the differences are unfavourable.

Managing Technological Resources

1. Technological resources are all the appropriate tools, equipment, technology, and facilities required to produce and deliver a product or service efficiently.

2. Big organisations can usually invest billions in capital-intensive production processes.

Class Activity 24.1 Business Proposal

Create a mini business proposal based on the research and business idea you have come up with in previous chapters. In your business proposal, you should do the following:

1. Convince any potential investor that your business venture is worth investing in.

2. Include presentation materials to be shown to potential investors, if necessary.

3. Describe the resources you would need to manage the business venture (human, physical, financial and technological).

4. Be as detailed as possible!

25 Problem-Solving

Define the steps in problem-solving within the workplace, including:

- Applying a decision-making process, such as SWOT analysis
- Identifying work-related problems and how to execute solutions

SWOT Analysis

1. There are various problem-solving tools and processes that can assist you in the workplace, such as the SWOT (strengths, weaknesses, opportunities, threats) analysis.

2. This process provides a snapshot of the internal strengths and weaknesses and external opportunities and threats surrounding **work-related problems** or any issue in general.

	Favourable	Unfavourable
Internal	**S** **Strengths** • What can you do well, and how have you demonstrated that you can do it well? • What can you offer to your potential employer?	**W** **Weaknesses** • What areas and skills are you not yet good at? • What do you need to improve on?
External	**O** **Opportunities** • What broader social and commercial trends are emerging? • What positive changes are happening in your industry or local geographical area?	**T** **Threats** • What external roadblocks could potentially prevent you from achieving your goals? • What are the negative changes in your industry or local geographical area?

Source: Adapted from Kenton (2021)

Figure 25.1 SWOT analysis looks at a combination of internal and external factors

Work-Related Problems

1. Some common problems in the workplace are summarised in Table 25.1.

Table 25.1   Work-related problems

Type of problem	Examples
Employee problems (including management staff)	• An employee being continually absent on busy days • A manager who acts aggressively towards subordinates
Customer/Client problems	• A customer who complains online about minor issues • A client who does not pay their bills
Equipment problems	• Outdated machinery that breaks down frequently • Equipment that is too complex to operate properly
Process problems	• Safety issues that are not adequately addressed • An online ordering system that fails to capture customer data and payments accurately

2. Other common work-related problems include:
    • Interpersonal conflicts
    • Communication breakdowns
    • Safety issues
    • Product faults and returns
    • Staff unavailability
    • Lack of staff training
    • Cost increases
    • Work-life imbalance
    • Environmental waste
    • New government regulations
    • Customer service problems
    • Stock shortages
    • Delivery issues
    • Profitability issues
    • Time-based issues
    • Manufacturing breakdowns

Class Activity 25.1 Business Proposal

Apply the SWOT analysis to your situation, using the following matrix as a guide.

Internal ╲ External	Opportunities	Threats
Strengths	*How do you leverage your strengths to benefit from opportunities?*	*How do you use your strengths to minimise the impact of threats?*
Weaknesses	*How do you ensure that your weaknesses do not hinder you from seizing opportunities?*	*How do you address your weaknesses that could make threats have a real impact?*

Homework 25.1 Work-Related Problem

Choose a work-related problem and develop an appropriate solution to address it. You may apply the SWOT analysis, if necessary.

You can use the space below to draft your solution.

_____

_____

_____

_____

_____

_____

_____

_____

_____

_____

_____

_____

_____

_____

_____

_____

_____

_____

_____

_____

_____

26 Conflict Resolution

Learning Objective

Describe strategies and processes for resolving conflicts in the workplace, including:

- Informal conflict resolution (such as communicating concerns to superiors or mentors, being tolerant of others and adopting internal mediation)
- Formal conflict resolution (such as arbitration, industrial tribunal hearings and trade union intervention)

Workplace Conflict

1. Conflicts may occur in the workplace due to poor interaction between colleagues or problems arising from work tasks. Such conflicts can result in stress, high labour turnover, low productivity, and poor relationships between parties, such as managers, employees, and customers.

2. Some examples of conflicts are as follows:

   - **Interpersonal conflict**
     Such conflicts might occur due to a clash of personalities, positions, responsibilities, values and attitudes. Many large organisations have conflict resolution procedures (grievance procedure) to tackle such clashes.

   - **Customer/client problems**
     Many employees face daily pressure and stress from difficult customers and clients. Employees dealing with customers should have conflict resolution training.

   - **Management/subordinate conflict**
     Some employees face conflict due to poor management and employee relations. Some managers are poorly trained and think that they can treat workers badly, while some workers have poor attitudes and feel they should not be told what to do.

   - **Personal/working-life conflict**
     Work hours, overtime, rosters, leave, deadlines, workload, stress, interpersonal relationships, and responsibilities have impact on our personal lives. We need to leave personal problems at home!

Informal Conflict Resolution

1. When a workplace conflict arises, the first step to resolving it is to employ informal strategies and processes. Those involved in the conflict can communicate their concerns to their superior or mentor.

2. Tolerance and a positive approach to resolving differences are critical to managing conflicts professionally. This ensures that the conflict does not persist and can be dealt with internally.

3. Internal mediation is an informal conflict resolution strategy where parties to a conflict have a dialogue about an issue. This allows the parties to address a problem directly, explore solutions and reach a satisfactory outcome.

Formal Conflict Resolution

1. When conflicts cannot be resolved informally, you as an employee can submit a formal complaint or grievance to initiate a formal conflict management process.

2. The following figure illustrates some formal conflict resolution strategies.

Figure 26.1   Formal conflict resolution strategies for dealing with conflicts in the workplace

Homework 26.1 Resolution Strategies

1. Research and discuss one of the formal conflict resolution strategies featured in the chapter.

2. Provide one conflict scenario where the strategy discussed is most appropriate.

Reflection 26.1 Conflict Resolution

1. Reflect on a conflict you have experienced before. Did you handle it well? If yes, why? If not, why not?

2. How did you resolve that conflict? Identify the conflict resolution process you employed (not necessarily related to the strategies listed in the chapter).

3. If you did not resolve that conflict satisfactorily, outline suggestions for improvements in future conflicts.

_____

_____

_____

_____

_____

_____

_____

_____

_____

_____

_____

_____

_____

_____

_____

27 Organisational Structures

Learning Objective

Describe key features of two organisational structures:
- Vertical
- Horizontal

Organisational Structures

1. An organisational structure refers to the organisation of an enterprise's responsibilities, employees, assets, and operations.

2. The structure also reflects the levels of authority, the degree of responsibility, and the accountability system of different management levels.

3. The two main organisational structures are the **vertical structure** and the **horizontal structure**.

Vertical Structure

1. The vertical organisational structure sets out the relationship between the levels of command to establish responsibility, authority and accountability within an organisation.

2. There are two types of vertical structure:

   - **Hierarchical (centralised)**
     The structure relies on a vertical chain of command to organise employees and their responsibilities. It is bureaucratic, with many management levels and vertical specialisations.

   - **Flat (decentralised)**
     Small companies mainly adopt this type of structure. It is organic and evolving with fewer management levels and more flexibility with crossover specialisation.

Horizontal Structure

1. The horizontal organisational structure sets out the departmental groupings within an organisation.

2. The grouping of tasks, employees and resources can be according to the following:
   - Function/operation
   - Geography/region
   - Division/product/market/department
   - Project/matrix

Function/Operation

1. This type of grouping organises employees based on the tasks performed. So, function or operation departmentalises an organisation according to standard job functions.

2. Employees have functional responsibility for their specialisation across all business activities. A sample chart depicting an organisational structure based on function or operation is given here.

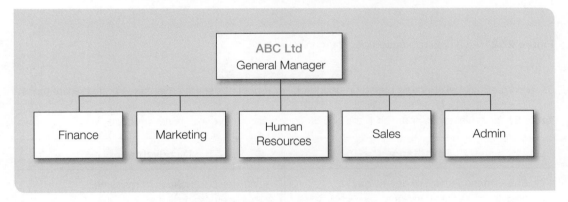

Figure 27.1   A sample of a functional organisational chart

3. An organisational structure based on function or operation has some advantages and disadvantages.

Table 27.1   Advantages and disadvantages of a functional organisational structure

Advantages	Disadvantages
• Experienced, specialised staff • Standardisation • Greater communication • Economies of scale due to efficiency	• Lack of variety • Lack of job fulfilment • Limits creativity and innovation • Bureaucratic due to a centralised structure

Geography/Region

1. This type of grouping is based on geographical locations or regions.

2. This is best suited to organisations that need to stay close to their customers or sources of supply (to facilitate deliveries and on-site support). A sample chart depicting an organisational structure based on geography or region is shown here.

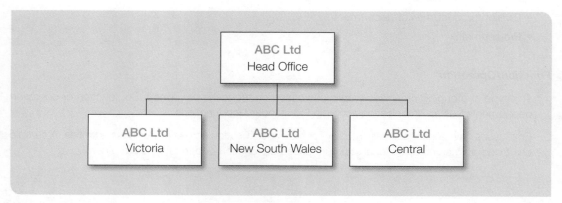

Figure 27.2   A sample of a geographical organisational chart

3. An organisational structure based on geography or region has some advantages and disadvantages.

Table 27.2   Advantages and disadvantages of a geographical organisational structure

Advantages	Disadvantages
• Easier management of day-to-day operations between regions • Better leverage of economic activities in local operations	• Wasteful duplication of resources between regions • Greater difficulty to maintain service consistency across geographical locations

Division/Product/Market/Department

1. This type of grouping organises employees based on output, putting together all necessary functional skills on managing a product line or customer group.

2. Managers with specialised functions are grouped according to their involvement in producing a product range or a specific consumer group. A sample chart depicting an organisational structure based on division, product, market or department is shown in the following page.

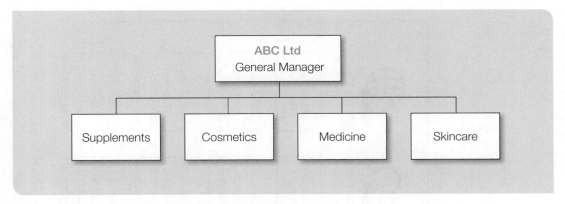

Figure 27.3   A sample of a divisional organisational chart

3. An organisational structure based on division, product, market or department has some advantages and disadvantages.

Table 27.3   Advantages and disadvantages of a divisional organisational structure

Advantages	Disadvantages
<ul><li>Friendly to fast-changing environments</li><li>High customer satisfaction as there is a clear contact point and product responsibility</li><li>High coordination across functions</li><li>Enabling of business units to adapt to variations in products, regions or customers</li><li>Decentralisation of decision-making power</li></ul>	<ul><li>No economies of scale</li><li>Poor coordination across different divisions</li><li>Lack of integration and standardisation across product lines or divisions</li><li>Limited achievement in in-depth competence and technical specialisation</li></ul>

Project/Matrix

1. This type of grouping is where the reporting relationships are set up as a grid—or matrix—rather than a traditional hierarchy.

2. In other words, employees have dual reporting relationships—generally, to both a functional manager and a product manager.

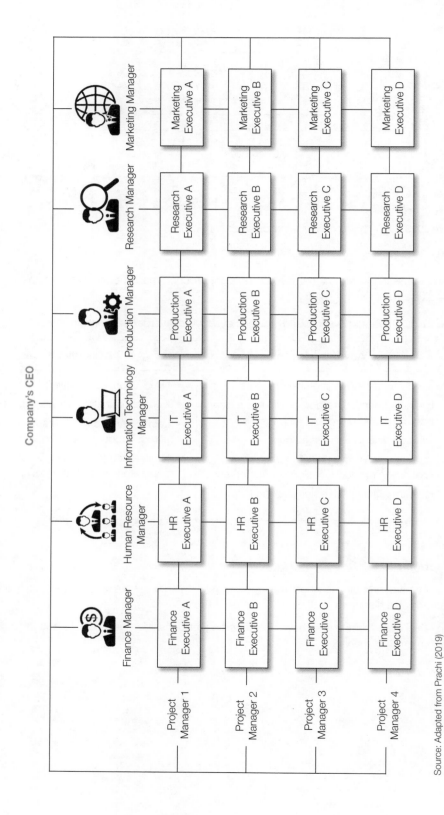

Source: Adapted from Prachi (2019)

Figure 27.4   A sample of a matrix organisational chart

3. A project/matrix organisational structure has some advantages and disadvantages.

Table 27.4   Advantages and disadvantages of a matrix organisational structure

Advantages	Disadvantages
• Greater diversity in work and thought process as different people from diverse departments work together • Improved professional development of employees as they are exposed to different functions apart from their core jobs • Higher productivity as more workers are involved in a project	• Ambiguity as to the reporting line • Confusion about role and responsibility • Difficult in gauging an employee's performance on a particular project • Less cost-efficient as more managers are employed

Homework 27.1 Organisational Structure Research

1. Research one organisational structure which has not been outlined in the chapter.

2. Write a description of the organisational structure and its advantages and disadvantages.

Organisational Structure	
Advantages	**Disadvantages**

28 Organisational Restructuring and Workplace Reform

Organisational Restructuring

1. Organisational restructuring aims to change how an organisation is structured to improve efficiency, quality and other performance-based outcomes.

2. It is a workplace reform process that promotes an enterprising culture to create greater economic productivity and more competitive industries, both locally and internationally. This may result in a significant change in the products, staffing requirement, ownership, or the original business model.

Workplace Reform

1. Workplace reform is an integrated approach to managing work to improve outcomes for work-related stakeholders.

2. It usually involves changing the structure of an organisation and redesigning how activities are carried out.

Class Activity 28.1 Workplace Reform Research

1. Research one example of organisational restructuring/workplace reform in Australia.

2. Research one example of organisational restructuring/workplace reform in another country apart from Australia.

3. Describe the restructuring/reform and investigate the reason(s) for such actions.

Reflection 28.1 How Do Reforms Impact Me?

In your journal, identify one organisational restructuring/workplace reform that you would be most impacted by, and explain why. You may link your journal entry with the job/industry you have selected previously.

_____

_____

_____

_____

_____

_____

_____

_____

_____

_____

_____

_____

_____

_____

_____

_____

_____

_____

_____

29 | Managing Changes

1. Describe the need to respond to change and ways to manage career changes, such as:
   - Retraining
   - Updating your skills
   - Improving your financial management

2. Recognise reasons for unemployment, including:
   - Mismatch of skills
   - Transitional changes

Managing Changes

1. "Change is the only constant" is a well-known phrase indicating the inevitability of change. Instead of resisting change, you can turn its pressures into opportunities by proactively managing the change well.

2. You can be proactive by recognising changes within your control and developing an action plan to respond to other changes outside your control. Some ways of managing career changes include **retraining**, **updating your skills** and **improving your financial management**.

   - **Retraining**
     Most of you will have a career lifespan of about 40 to 50 years and will need to learn a few new skills over time. Retraining and even lifelong learning will give you skills that will stay relevant throughout your career.

   - **Updating your skills**
     The skills you acquired before starting your first job may become outdated over time. You should always consider updating your skills based on the latest developments to keep yourself up-to-date in the field and remain competitive. This is particularly crucial for technological skills, which require constant updates.

   - **Managing your financial management**
     It is vital to develop some skills in financial management to deal with changes affecting your career. Getting your first pay cheque is indeed a satisfying feeling; however, it is essential to manage your finances from the start of your career to avoid having financial difficulties in the future.

Unemployment

1. Unemployment is when you cannot find a job despite actively seeking one.

2. Unemployment can happen for various reasons, the most common being a **mismatch of skills** and **transitional changes** in your life or career.
   - **Mismatch of skills**
     This refers to discrepancies between your skills and the skills in demand in the working world.
   - **Transitional changes**
     Transitional changes occur when you graduate from university, when the company you work in undergoes organisational restructures, or when your contract or temporary position ends.

Class Activity 29.1 Retraining and Skills Update

1. Discuss some examples of skills that you think will require retraining or updating.

2. Provide a few ways of retraining and updating your skills.

Homework 29.1 Budget Planner

1. Prepare a budget planner to forecast a weekly/monthly budget for yourself.

2. You may research and look for available templates online, and use the one you find most suitable.

Reflection 29.1 Transitions

1. Identify two transitions that you are likely to experience in your career (soon and in the future).

2. Write a reflection on the following question in your journal: "Why are transitions good for me?"

30 Efficiency and Sustainability

Efficiency

1. Efficiency is the ability to perform an intended job with zero or little waste of resources, energy and time. Various key performance indicators can be used to assess your efficiency in work-related situations.

2. Efficiency is difficult to measure. It depends on your assessment of what you gain from work and how the work meets expectations.

3. The more efficient you are, the more likely you feel satisfied with yourself and your work. Some intrinsic factors that lead to job satisfaction include:

   - Recognition and reward
   - Opportunity for advancement and career development
   - Improved skills and competencies
   - Sense of pride, self-respect and self-esteem

4. With efficiency and job satisfaction, your productivity level will increase. This will also increase the productivity level of the company you work in.

Sustainability

1. Sustainability involves reducing the use of non-renewable resources in favour of renewable resources. This is to preserve natural resources and avoid irreversible environmental effects on the planet.

2. Carbon footprint reduction is one of the main ways to minimise consumption of non-renewable resources (e.g. coal and oil). This can include measures such as:

   - Conserving electricity
   - Reducing paper usage
   - Recycling
   - Organic farming

3. Sustainability and eco-friendly habits in the workplace are not only good for the environment; they also help businesses reduce their overheads, safeguard the health of employees, and attract customers looking for eco-friendly brands.

Class Activity 30.1 Efficiency

Discuss ways to increase efficiency at work.

Homework 30.1 Sustainability: SDG Research

Research the 17 Sustainable Development Goals (SDGs) by the United Nations and present your findings in your own words.

More information on the SDGs can be found at https://sdgs.un.org/goals

Goal	Description
1. No poverty	
2. Zero hunger	

Goal	Description
3. Good health and well-being	
4. Quality education	
5. Gender equality	
6. Clean water and sanitation	
7. Affordable and clean energy	

Goal	Description
8. Decent work and economic growth	
9. Industry, innovation and infrastructure	
10. Reduced inequality	
11. Sustainable cities and communities	
12. Responsible consumption and production	

Goal	Description
13. Climate action	
14. Life below water	
15. Life on land	
16. Peace, justice and strong institutions	
17. Partnerships for the goals	

31 | Health and Safety

1. Recognise the need for health and safety at the workplace
2. Identify the stakeholders of workplace health and safety

Health and Safety

1. Workplace Health and Safety (WHS) is the general term used to describe the rights, responsibilities, training, regulations, guidelines, laws and other issues related to ensuring a safe work environment.

2. Health and safety at the workplace are a shared responsibility and WHS stakeholders play an essential role in maintaining safe work practices.

WHS Stakeholders

1. **Employees**
   - Employees perform tasks and duties and have a fundamental right to a safe workplace
   - They also have a responsibility to perform work safely and replace or remove any hazards

2. **Employers**
   - Employers design work environments and implement and supervise work practices
   - They must do so with utmost care and concern for the safety of employees and stakeholders. This is required by law!

3. **Government**
   - The government controls and enforces most WHS laws and guidelines (e.g. WorkSafe in WA)
   - Safe Work Australia is the national body that develops model work health and safety laws

4. **Unions**
   - Unions play a proactive and leading role in developing WHS policies, guidelines and laws throughout the industry
   - They work with the government, employers and employees to ensure that workers have access to a safe workplace

5. **WHS officer**
   - Many workplaces have an official WHS officer responsible for monitoring and maintaining safe conditions for workers
   - The WHS officer usually acts as a go-between for employees and management

6. **WHS consultants/inspectors**
   - WHS consultants or inspectors are external specialists contracted to assess an organisation or work setting for WHS risks
   - They might also represent their local WHS authority, which gives them the power to deal with issues related to WHS
   - They help employers design and implement work environments and practices that minimise harm
   - They can also train employees and management in WHS issues

Class Activity 31.1   SmartMove Certificate

1. Visit https://smartmove.safetyline.wa.gov.au/certificate and complete the General Module and one Industry Module.

2. Investigate three recently developed safe work practices worldwide due to the COVID-19 pandemic.

_____

_____

_____

_____

_____

_____

_____

_____

_____

_____

_____

_____

_____

32 Work Rights

Pay and Conditions

1. In making a career choice, several factors are often considered:
   - Wages and salaries
   - Leave entitlements
   - Superannuation
   - Fringe benefits
   - Workplace perks
   - Allowances

2. In Australia, the Fair Work Act 2009 is a law to reform the industrial relations system in the country, commencing 1 July 2009. Under the law, all employees are entitled to the National Employment Standards (NES) which list 11 minimum terms and conditions of employment. The NES makes up a safety net that cannot be altered to the employee's disadvantage.

3. The 11 minimum conditions covered under the NES are as follows:

- Maximum of 38 weekly hours of work
- Requests for flexible work arrangements
- Offers and requests to convert from casual to permanent employment
- Parental leave and related entitlements
- Annual leave
- Personal or carer's leave and compassionate leave
- Community service leave
- Long service leave
- Public holidays
- Notice of termination and redundancy pay
- A fair work information statement

Source: Fair Work Commission (n.d.)

Ethics and Code of Conduct

1. Ethics are a set of rules prescribed to guide your actions and behaviour. In the workplace, ethical management is associated with doing "the right things right".

2. Employees are also expected to adhere to codes of conduct at work. These codes—governed by laws such as the Equal Opportunity Act 1984, Fair Trading Act 2010 and Workplace Health and Safety regulations—are embedded in the organisational culture via induction programmes.

Workplace Technology

1. Rapid technological advancement has driven many workplace changes, resulting in improved work-related outcomes.

2. However, the use of workplace technology has raised several issues:

   - **Safety**
     Data security and hazards.

   - **Environmental**
     Disposal of e-waste.

   - **Ethical**
     Data privacy.

3. Employees need to be aware of the expectations, protocols and legal requirements surrounding the use of technology in the workplace:

   - Licensing, registration and compliance
   - Age restrictions on handling machinery
   - Privacy laws
   - Intellectual property laws (e.g. trademark, patent and copyright)

Quality Assurance

1. Quality assurance is a process in which an organisation receives recognition on its systems and processes that meet national and international quality standards, such as Standards Australia and the International Standards Organisation.

2. Such recognition acts as a quality guarantee and can help increase confidence in the organisation among stakeholders.

Class Activity 32.1 Work Rights Research

1. Visit https://www.fairwork.gov.au/employee-entitlements/national-employment-standards and find out more details about the 11 minimum conditions covered under the National Employment Standards from the Fair Work Act 2009.

2. Conduct brief research and compare Standards Australia and International Standards Association Organisation.

Homework 32.1 Workplace Technology Legislations

1. Identify several relevant legislations for workplace technology regarding safety, environmental and ethical issues.

2. In one sentence, briefly describe the purpose of each legislation.

_____

_____

_____

_____

_____

_____

_____

_____

_____

_____

FURTHER READING

Fair Work Commission. (n.d.). National employment standards. https://www.fwc.gov.au/awards-and-agreements/minimum-wages-conditions/national-employment-standards

Carolan, M. (2016). Career and enterprise: CAE—General 12 / ATAR 11. Deliver Educational Consulting.

Corporate Finance Institute. (n.d.). SMART goal: Specific, measurable, attainable, realistic, timely. https://corporatefinanceinstitute.com/resources/knowledge/other/smart-goal

Holland, J. L. (1985). Making vocational choices: A theory of vocational personalities and work environments (2nd ed.). Prentice-Hall.

Job Outlook. (n.d.). Explore industries. https://joboutlook.gov.au/industries

Kenton, W. (2021, March 30). Strength, weakness, opportunity, and threat (SWOT) analysis. Investopedia. https://www.investopedia.com/terms/s/swot.asp

Miles, L. R. M., & Roe, M. (2008). Career and enterprise: A resource for units 2A and 2B. Impact Publishing.

Southam, K. (n.d.). Improve your interview technique: Better screening methods for potential candidates. CareerOne. https://hiring.careerone.com.au/hiring-advice/recruiting-hiring-advice/improve-your-interview-technique

Prachi, M. (2019). Matrix organizational structure. The Investors Book. https://theinvestorsbook.com/matrix-organizational-structure.html

Truity. (n.d.). How to use Holland codes to find the right career. https://www.truity.com/page/holland-code-riasec-theory-career-choice

ACKNOWLEDGEMENTS

Writing a book has been more rewarding than I could have ever imagined. It would not have been possible without the support of my former colleague, Sophia Ngiaw Yeng Fern. She was the subject leader of the Career and Enterprise Year 12 General course when it was first introduced in the Australian Matriculation (AUSMAT) programme at Sunway College Kuala Lumpur, Malaysia. She was instrumental in developing the curriculum content delivery to students. When I had the opportunity to teach this subject, she was an excellent thought partner and mentor. During the book writing process, she kindly reviewed my draft and provided valuable ideas and input, for which I am eternally grateful.

I would also like to express my gratitude to Ms Vanitha Satchithanadan, the programme director for AUSMAT and the assistant director of Sunway College's Pre-University Studies, who has been a constant source of support and guidance in my personal and professional development. She has been one of those leaders who has inspired me to pursue new challenges and opportunities. This book would not have been published without her unwavering support.

My heartfelt appreciation also goes to AUSMAT Sunway, the AUSMAZING team, who demonstrates a can-do culture and passion for excellence. All of you have my most profound respect and are my source of inspiration in my endeavours to be a better educator.

Undeniably, the publication of this book could not have materialised without Sunway University Press. One person in particular who deserves a special mention is the editor, Hani Hazman, who had been exceptionally professional in the editing, reviewing, and publishing process. She patiently assisted me in enhancing the quality of this book with her expertise throughout this journey. Thank you very much, Hani.

To my wife, Serene, your unconditional love and support during this entire time is something that I truly cherish for the rest of my life. To my family and friends, who have always been there for me, I thank God for each one of you. Praise the Lord!